FENG SHUI
AT
WORK

FENG SHUI
AT
WORK

*Attracting prosperity
and success to your
workplace*

ANTONIA BEATTIE

CONSULTANT – ROSEMARY STEVENS

LANSDOWNE

CONTENTS

INTRODUCTION

A substantial salary, a desired promotion and a fulfilling and interesting career are all possible if the Chinese art of placement called 'feng shui' is observed in your workplace and home.

The idea of an invisible life force or energy was developed in a number of ancient civilizations, including China, many centuries ago. In feng shui, this energy (known as 'qi') has the force of the wind ('feng'), flows like water ('shui') and is connected to every living organism.

In China, it is believed that this energy can either flow or stagnate according to the shape and form of your surroundings, both natural and artificial. If it is allowed to flow at a gentle, steady pace, it brings great benefits, such as good fortune and success in business. If it is allowed to stagnate or move too fast, the energy may bring with it bankruptcy, legal worries and poor luck.

Like wind and water, this energy can be manipulated to flow beneficially using the art of feng shui, which focuses on using or blocking the energy generated by the environment surrounding your place of business and your personal work space. For example, bad energy can be blocked simply by moving a piece of furniture in a particular direction and good energy can be stimulated by placing a few coins on a certain part of your work table.

It is not only the physical surroundings of your workplace and home that affect the flow of energy. Feng shui practitioners also believe that the name of your company, the street number of your premises and your company logo may attract or block beneficial energy.

Once you understand the flow of energy around you and your workplace, you will find it easy to make a few small changes that will make a difference to the quality and quantity of your work and to the profits of your business.

Feng shui is a very effective form of energy control because it helps us strengthen our connection with nature. By understanding and tapping into the flow of life energy, we can link into nature's powerful balance and harmony, transforming our workplaces and homes into efficient conductors of that energy.

This book will help you to understand and apply the main principles of feng shui. While there are a number of different schools of feng shui, the purpose of this book is to eliminate the confusion and provide a simplified practice of feng shui, giving you an understanding of the main principles. You can then use these to explore this ancient system more deeply.

WHAT YOU NEED TO KNOW ABOUT FENG SHUI

~

TAPPING INTO THE POWERFUL FLOW OF LIFE ENERGY

Many civilizations, ancient and modern, believe that there is an invisible, universal energy which flows around us. In China, this is called qi. It is believed that it flows through and around all matter, and that there is a strong connection between the the flow of this energy and our wellbeing and prosperity.

In Chinese mythology, this energy is said to be created by a powerful cosmic green dragon who made his lair in a hilly terrain. All gently undulating hills are associated with the dragon's energy and it is believed that this type of landscape, including gently flowing watercourses in the valleys, is particularly auspicious energy.

The best spot for a house was believed to be near (but not too near) the dragon's lair, generally halfway between the top of the hill and the valley, with the back of the house cradled by the hill. This position makes the most of the combination of descending heaven qi and ascending earth qi.

Heaven qi is the energy that flows around the planets, the clouds and wind. It is believed that the weather is caused by the various moods of the dragon; for instance, thunderstorms occur when it is feeling angry. Earth qi is the energy of both the natural and artificial environment, so it includes both mountains and skyscrapers. There is also human qi, which is generated between people, as well as personal qi, which reflects the energy that moves through your body, thoughts and personality.

ENERGY AT YOUR DOORSTEP

Beneficial qi comes from the south and so the main entrance of your business should ideally be positioned there. However, if you run your own business, you may wish to consider placing the door at a direction which suits your personal qi (see pages 62–71).

It is important for the different types of qi to flow gently, freely and without impediment, much like the flow of water in a slow, meandering river. If energy is allowed to do this, it brings benefits to the people near it. This beneficial qi is known as 'sheng qi'. If the qi is blocked, stagnant or is made to move too quickly, particularly through long, straight streets without trees lining the sidewalk, it turns into a negative form of energy called 'sha qi'. Sha qi can also be created by sharp corners, both in the shape of a room and in prominent pieces of furniture. This form of sha qi is called 'secret' or 'poison arrows'.

THE DYNAMIC OF YIN AND YANG

In feng shui, as in Chinese medicine and philosophy, the life force, qi, is stimulated by the balance between two opposing forces, yin and yang. Yin and yang are not precisely defined, but at their most basic level, yin is female or introverted energy, while yang is male or extroverted energy.

Symbolically, yin and yang are represented by the colors black and white within a circle, gently swirling around each other. The black symbolizes yin and the white symbolizes yang. Each one contains a tiny drop of the opposing color, symbolizing that each force contains a small amount of the other.

Yin and yang forces both attract and repel one another. This constant 'struggle' between them moves qi through the universe, and everything in the universe can be categorized as containing either yin or yang energies or characteristics. Once yin and yang components are in balance, then the life force is also in balance, which leads to a sense of wellbeing and prosperity in a person's life.

In feng shui, yin and yang must be in harmony to make sure that qi flows beneficially through an interior. Yin energy is expressed by using dark gray, blue and green colors, and in the space between pieces of furniture in the area. Yin energy is also inherent in curved walls. Yang energy is expressed with bright, warm colors and is found within the furniture in the room, as well as in straight walls. It is important that there is a balance between dark and bright colors, space and furniture, and curved and straight walls.

If your office is too yin, you may find the room depressing and uncomfortable and that you do not meet your work commitments because you are feeling too lethargic. To correct this, place a warmly colored cushion, seat cover or picture in the office and check your lighting. You may even wish to paint the walls white.

If your office is too yang, you may find that you feel overworked and suffer from severe headaches, accidents and an inability to focus. If you have too much clutter and too many bright lights and colors around you, reduce the number of books, files and furniture in your office, and introduce cool colors and a few potted plants.

Yin	Yang
Female	Male
Introvert	Extrovert
Negative	Positive
Black	White
Soft	Hard
Curved	Straight
Night	Day
New moon	Full moon
Wet	Dry
Sugar	Salt

HOW NATURE AFFECTS THE OFFICE:
THE ROLE OF THE ELEMENTS

We often think of ourselves being very far removed from nature, especially if we work in a big city or town. Nevertheless, according to Chinese beliefs we, like the rest of our world, are made up of five natural elements which correspond to a particular direction and energy.

Element	Direction	Type of energy
Wood	East	Unpredictable yet exciting
Fire	South	Active and expansive
Earth	Center	Balanced and mature
Metal	West	Demanding yet rewarding
Water	North	Quiet and isolated

The year of birth indicates which element is predominant in someone's personality. In the table below, the last digit of your year of birth indicates your dominant element for the Chinese solar year (see pages 78–79) and whether you are a yang or a yin type. What type of work is attractive to you is also noted:

Last digit of year of birth	Element	Yin/yang	Work style
1	Metal	Yin	Prefers to have everything in order
2	Water	Yang	Prefers to be an independent consultant
3	Water	Yin	Prefers to work quietly and alone
4	Wood	Yang	Prefers to work in a competitive environment
5	Wood	Yin	Prefers to have a heavy workload
6	Fire	Yang	Prefers to work in a team
7	Fire	Yin	Prefers to use their intuition
8	Earth	Yang	Prefers to work long-term for one employer
9	Earth	Yin	Prefers to work in harmony with co-workers
0	Metal	Yang	Prefers to organize and be in charge

The elements affect each other, and this can be productive or negative. Follow the arrows of the illustration below to understand the relationship between the elements. The outer circle running clockwise indicates the creative or yang relationship between the elements – wood helps feed fire, the fire of the sun nourishes the earth, earth contains seams of metal, metal objects can be a receptacle for water and water nourishes wood. The inner five-pointed star indicates the destructive or yin relationship between the elements – wood hinders earth, earth muddies water, water puts out fire, fire melts metal and metal chops down wood.

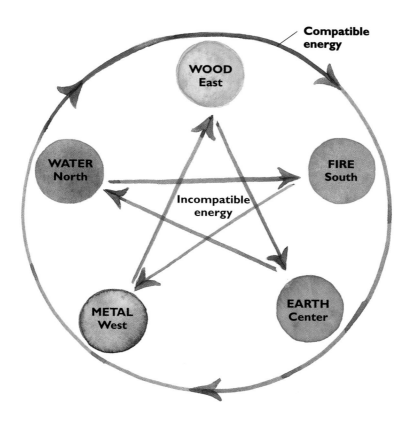

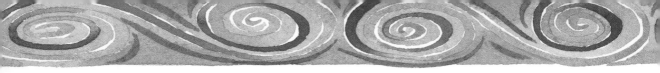

THE EIGHT ASPIRATIONS OF LIFE

In feng shui, there are eight aspirations of life, listed in the table opposite. To start the practice of feng shui, you must determine which area of your place of business or home corresponds with which aspiration. There are a number of ways of doing this, which can make the practice of feng shui seem particularly difficult and confusing.

However, the simplest way of attributing the eight aspirations is to subdivide your building into nine equal boxes – the magic square (see pages 22–23). The middle box corresponds to the earth and no aspiration is attributed to it. However, it does represent the general state of your building. The magic square is positioned according to where your main entrance is. No matter how many entrances and windows you have in your building, qi flows in through the main front door.

Another way of discovering how the aspirations correspond with your building is to find out which direction the building faces. Each of the eight main directions of the compass corresponds to a particular aspiration (see the table opposite).

EXPERT ADVICE

The aspirations may be attributed to your entire building or to your office space and even to your work bench, desk or retail counter.

Aspiration	Corresponding number	Directions
Wealth	4	Southeast
Acknowledgment & fame	9	South
Relationships	2	Southwest
Family and health	3	East
Children and creativity	7	West
Education	8	Northeast
Career	1	North
Mentors and travel	6	Northwest

REMEDYING THE POOR FLOW OF LIFE ENERGY:
FENG SHUI CURES

Feng shui cures are the simplest ways of correcting any stagnation or fast movement of qi through your building or office space. These cures are basically symbols, such as coins, tassels and fans, that metaphysically force fast-moving qi to slow down or encourage stagnant qi to move in a beneficial way. They can also be used to block harmful energy and can be manipulated to enhance the energy in a particular area of a building, such as the wealth sector.

There are several levels of cures. One level focuses on the correspondences between the eight aspirations and the elements (see also pages 12–13). Each element resonates with a particular direction and consequently with an aspiration. To enhance the circulation of qi within the area of the aspiration, objects made of the relevant element should be placed in the corresponding area and any objects made of elements that are destructive to that aspiration's element should be removed.

For example, you should place items made of wood in the wealth aspiration area of your building, office space or work table, because the wood element corresponds with wealth. Water also corresponds with wealth because water nurtures wood. However, do not place any metal in the area, as metal can cut down wood (old Chinese coins strung together with red thread are the exception). For the productive and destructive relationship between the elements, see the illustration on page 13.

Another level of cures symbolize the balancing of forms and yin and yang energies to correct the flow of qi. The table below lists both elemental corrections and other traditional feng shui cures.

Aspiration	Elements and feng shui cures to include	Elements to avoid
Wealth	Wood, water, plants and pets	Metal
Acknowledgment & fame	Wood, fire, lights and mirrors	Water
Relationships	Wood, fire, mobiles and flags	Water
Family and health	Wood, water, fans and flutes	Metal
Creativity and children	Metal, earth, solid objects, statues and rocks	Fire
Knowledge	Water, metal and sound	Earth
Career	Water, metal and bright colors	Earth
Mentors and travel	Metal, earth, chimes and bells	Fire

YOU AND FENG SHUI

Follow your feelings when applying the principles of feng shui to your workplace. Your intuition is an important aspect of the practice of feng shui. Trust your feelings about the flow of energy in your workplace. Before subdividing the building, your office space or your work table into the eight aspirations (pages 14–15), walk around both the outside and the inside of the building.

As you walk around, notice where clutter has collected, where accidents have occurred, where arguments have broken out and where the building or rooms show signs of neglect or disrepair. These are all signs of either the stagnation or overly strong presence of qi.

Many of us, to some degree or other, have a feeling about what would look 'right' in a particular room, although we may not know why. The placement of a potted palm in a certain corner may seem satisfying, even though we don't realize that the plant now shields us from a poison arrow created by a protruding corner.

Clutter, garbage and other examples of neglect are signs of either stagnation or an overly strong presence of qi.

At times, though, there may be some areas that 'just don't work', no matter what we do. This is where feng shui becomes particularly useful, as it can help you identify where the qi is stagnating and choose the solution that will help qi flow harmoniously through your building.

It is also beneficial to use your intuition to determine how many feng shui cures (see pages 16–17) you are going to use at once. Make the most appropriate changes and allow a period of time to elapse to see if you can feel any subtle results in the area. Make sure that you only use a few cures at a time, since too many cures may become clutter in themselves.

Often the clutter of a room may be an indication of a cluttered mind or disorganized work. Try to eliminate the unnecessary clutter in your office by deciding what you really need to have in your work space. Doing so stimulates your mind to do the same, allowing you to focus more clearly on finding success and fulfillment in your business.

If you wish to stimulate one of the eight aspirations for yourself only, you may place an object in the area to which the aspiration corresponds. This object should be made from an element that relates to your dominant personality element. Go back to the chart on pages 12–13 to identify which element dominates your personality. For more information on how you interact with your work environment, see pages 62–67.

APPLYING FENG SHUI

~

FENG SHUI SCHOOLS OF THOUGHT

There are three schools of feng shui: bagua feng shui, compass feng shui and form feng shui. In this book, we will be concentrating on bagua feng shui, which involves working out a nine-square grid ('the magic square'). However, elements of both the compass and form schools will also be incorporated.

Each of the eight outer sections of the magic square is attributed to an aspiration, while the central sector is attributed to the earth element. The earth element indicates the potential of the business.

There are two simple ways of using the magic square or grid. The simplest way is to align the grid according to where your main entrance is (see pages 22–23). The second method is to align the grid with the building's orientation. See pages 24–25 to find out how to use a compass to work out the orientation of your building. See pages 26–27 to find out how to align the feng shui grid with your building plans in relation to the eight compass directions.

To understand the relationship between you and your workplace, first determine whether your personal orientation suits the orientation of your workplace or place of business. This form of calculation is part of the compass school of feng shui, which concentrates on distinguishing between east and west types of people and buildings.

It is believed that if you are a west type of person, you will feel most comfortable and be most successful in a west type of building. If you are an east type of person, an east group workplace will suit you best. A building is east or west according to its orientation (see pages 24–25). Whether you belong to the east or west group depends upon certain calculations, and these are different for men and women (see pages 62–65).

The compass school uses a number of complex calculations as well as Chinese astrology and a special feng shui compass called the luo-pan. The luo-pan is a flat disc containing a Western-style compass surrounded by a series of concentric circles which identify the correspondences between the elements, compass directions and other important correspondences.

The form school concentrates on the flow of qi in the environment, and emphasises the shape of the surroundings of your building and the position of your building relative to conductors of qi such as roads, rivers and mountains (see pages 28–35).

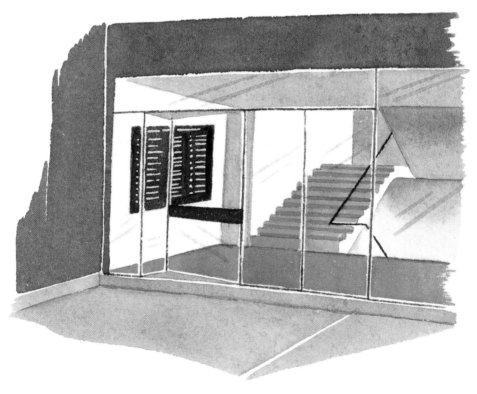

THE MAGIC SQUARE: A SIMPLE GRID CALCULATION

The magic square or luo-shu is one of the simplest ways of working out which areas of your workplace correspond with each feng shui aspiration (see pages 14–15). This square is also referred to as the bagua or pa-kwa.

The square contains a sequence of numbers. The first sequence, called the former heaven sequence, is now rarely used. The later heaven sequence is now most commonly used. The formation of numbers was said to have been found on the back of a huge turtle. The back of the turtle's shell was divided equally into nine squares and each square contained an arrangement of dots, ranging from one to nine. Each number corresponded with an aspiration.

Follow these easy steps to find out where the different aspirations fall within your building, work space or table:

• Obtain or draw a floor plan of your building.

• Draw a regular square or rectangle around the perimeter of your building. Ignore minor projections outside this regular shape or any missing areas for this exercise; just try to make your building fit into a regular shape.

• On a separate piece of paper, trace the shape of your building and then subdivide it into nine roughly equal sections. Write the aspirations in the same squares as the following grid:

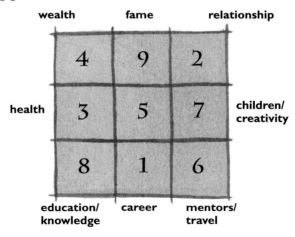

• Note where your main entrance is and align the bottom of the grid (with the aspirations, from left to right, of *Education*, *Career* and *Mentors*) with the wall on your plan containing your main entrance. You do not need to worry about compass directions with this system.

You will find that if your building is not symmetrical and there is a section missing in your plan, you may experience some difficulties in the corresponding aspiration of your business's life. If there is a minor protrusion (less than a third of the length of the building) in a particular aspiration, it can have the reverse effect; that is, the area may experience some benefits and good luck.

If the projection is quite substantial (for example, a room causes your building to be L-shaped), you may experience some disruptions in the aspiration area to which the projection is attached and may have to remedy the poison arrows generated by the corner of the 'L'.

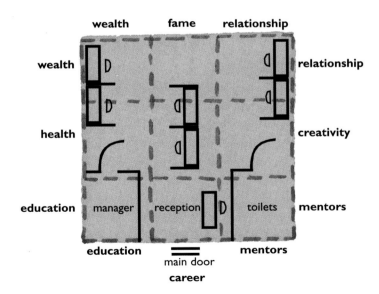

USING A COMPASS TO FIND THE ORIENTATION
OF YOUR BUILDING

To find out if your workplace has an eastern or western orientation, you can use a standard Western compass. The best way to work out your building's orientation is to determine its sitting direction; that is, the compass direction in which the back of the building faces.

In offices which are part of a larger commercial building, it is important to work out the sitting direction of the building where your office is and the relationship of your office to the building. For instance, your office building may be sitting in the west, while the main entrance to your office faces towards the back of the building. The sitting position of your office is still in the west, even though the main entrance of your office faces the building's sitting position.

If the building is sitting in the following compass directions, its orientation is to the east:

- East
- Southeast
- South
- North

EXPERT ADVICE

Sometimes it can be difficult to get an accurate compass reading at the back of the workplace. This can be due to a number of reasons, such as electrical interference. If this is the case, go to the front of the building and take a compass reading. If you still cannot get a reading, go inside the building and take the measurement facing the main entrance or with your back to the back entrance.

If the building is sitting in the following compass directions, its orientation is to the west:

- West
- Northwest
- Southwest
- Northeast

To work out your building's orientation with a compass, stand with your back against the back wall of the building (the wall as far back from the main entrance as possible). Align your compass to the north and then read the compass grade to work out which way the back of the building is facing. Use the table below to work out what your compass grade means:

Compass grade	Sitting direction
22.5 - 67.5	Northeast
67.5 - 112.5	East
112.5 - 157.5	Southeast
157.5 - 202.5	South
202.5 - 247.5	Southwest
247.5 - 292.5	West
292.2 - 337.5	Northwest
337.5 - 22.5	North

THE BAGUA

The bagua or pa-kwa is an octagonal picture or object that contains a trigram in each of its eight sides and an image of the yin/yang symbol in the center. The yin/yang symbol represents the element of earth. A trigram is a 'picture' of three lines stacked one upon the other. Each side of the octagonal bagua also represents the eight compass directions, giving a corresponding trigram, number and compass direction to each of the eight aspirations (see pages 14–15).

The lines of the trigram are either broken or unbroken. The broken lines correspond with yin or introverted energy and the unbroken lines correspond with yang or extroverted energy. There are two types of sequences, called the former heaven sequence and the later heaven sequence. In each sequence, the positioning of the aspirations according to the bagua is different. The former heaven sequence is illustrated below.

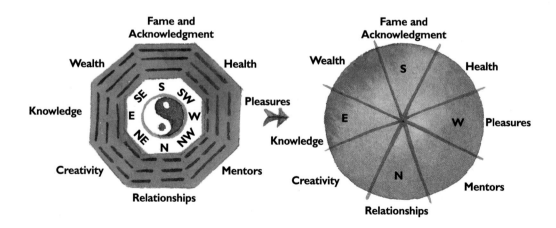

These eight trigrams, which were apparently observed on a horse standing at the Lo River, are thought to be the precursors to the sixty-four trigrams used in the I-Ching or Book of Changes. The I-Ching is used as a form of divination and was devised over 3,000 years ago. With the development of the I-Ching, the sequence of the trigrams was altered and developed into the later heaven sequence, which is now the most commonly used for bagua readings.

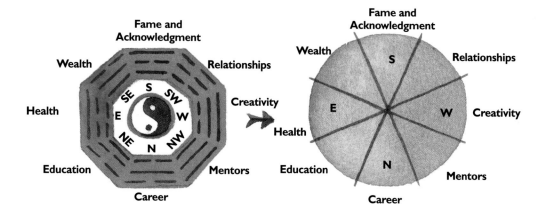

To relate the bagua to your workplace, sketch or find a plan of your workplace and draw lines around the plan which will make it a symmetrical square or rectangle if it is not already. Follow the instructions of how to find the orientation of your building on pages 24–25. Draw through the middle of the plan or sketch a line that indicates the north and south axis and then draw a perpendicular line through the middle to indicate the east and west axis.

On a separate piece of paper, preferably thin, transparent paper, draw a circle which is slightly larger than the shape of your plan. Subdivide the circle into the eight sections described above and corresponding aspirations. This is your bagua. Align the middle of the north section of the bagua along the line on your plan indicating your north and south axis.

WHAT SHAPE IS YOUR WORKPLACE IN?

~

WHAT DOES THE SHAPE OF YOUR BUILDING MEAN?

Balance and symmetry are important aspects of feng shui. Square or rectangular buildings are considered most beneficial for the best flow of qi. A square is related to the earth element and gives its occupants a sense of stability and endurance, while rectangles correspond with the wood element and are symbolic of growth and resilience.

The form school of feng shui believes that the regular shapes of a square or a rectangle do not create sharp angles where qi has difficulty flowing in and out. This is a problem with triangular buildings or plots of land. The inability of qi to flow freely leads to stagnation, which in turn leads to the creation of 'poison arrows' of negative energy which can be very detrimental to your business or career prospects.

Shapes related to the elements of fire, water and metal are not auspiciously formed to provide the occupants with the best flow of qi. The flow of qi in triangular buildings is as unpredictable as fire, and the top of the triangle creates a great deal of negative or sha qi. Circular buildings, which are related to the element of metal, are believed to create swirls of energy that are too strong, overwhelming the occupants and causing headaches and a lack of focus. Buildings that correspond to the element of water always strike the observer as a jumbled mess of shapes, causing an up-and-down flow of qi which also causes an unstable sensation.

Buildings whose shape corresponds with the shape of their environment are the most stable. However, for a prosperous life, the following combinations are ideal:

• A building made of concrete and bricks (earth) is best suited to mountainous terrain (fire).

• A large-scale metal skyscraper (metal) is best situated near large bodies of water (water).

• A building of irregular shapes and sizes (water) is best situated near a rounded hillside or large-scale metal buildings (metal).

• A house with a sharp roof line (fire) is best situated near a large park (wood).

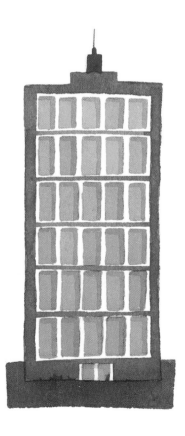

EXPERT ADVICE

A building that incorporated a number of metal cones as a design feature was experiencing a lot of bad luck, as the tips of the cones were directing poison arrows at a nature reserve. The metal element, represented by the cones, clashed strongly with the forest, which represented the element of wood. This clash created very bad luck within the building. External water ponds were especially made to break the destructive connection between metal and wood, and this cleared the bad energy by replicating the constructive flow of qi between the elements of metal, water and wood (see pages 12–13).

THE SHAPE OF THE ENVIRONMENT AROUND YOUR BUILDING

The form school of feng shui believes that the shape of the environment is very important for directing the right kind of qi towards your building and business. According to ancient Chinese mythology, four celestial beasts represent four aspects of the environment, and it is important that a building is positioned so that the natural protection afforded by these beasts is activated.

The four directions around a building are symbolized by the crimson phoenix in the south, the black turtle in the north, the white tiger in the west and the azure dragon in the east. These represent the four major divisions of the macro-constellations in Chinese astrology. The balance between heaven qi and earth qi is symbolized by these celestial creatures, which form a protective guard around your building.

To enhance the protection of these celestial creatures, the front of a building should ideally face north. North corresponds with the element of water, which is represented by the flow of traffic along the roadway in front of a building. The back of the building should face south. South resonates with the element of fire, which is represented by a hill.

This hill provides protection and support to a business. If you have no hill behind you and your business is suffering some bad luck, place four or eight earthenware pots in a row outside your back door. Number eight represents mountains, while number four represents wood. Wood or a forest behind your building also gives support to the business. It is believed to be very inauspicious for a hill to be positioned at the front of the building, as it leads to stagnation and oppression.

The west, which relates to the element of metal, corresponds to rounded

EXPERT ADVICE

If you have a hill or rise of land directly in front of your main entrance, soften the area with curves and plants and filter the view with a screen or lattice and a vine. Also, install upward external lighting to make the building appear taller. This is a necessary precaution, even if your building is already taller than the rise in front of your main entrance.

hills or, in modern terms, metal high-rise buildings, while the east relates to the element of wood and corresponds to parkland and forests.

The best position for a business building is in the middle of a gently sloping hillside, with the hill rising behind it and an unobstructed view to the plains, and a lake, harbor or meandering river in front.

Working on the top of a hill can make you feel vulnerable to the elements and exposed to the harsher elements of life, while working at the bottom of a hill may feel (and in fact, it is) overwhelmingly dangerous, because the energy flowing straight down the mountain will have created a poison arrow by the time it hits the base of the mountain. Living on a flat area was traditionally considered inauspicious, but it is no longer thought to be problematic.

POSITION, POSITION, POSITION:
THE IMPORTANCE OF LOCATION

One of the most important aspects of feng shui is making sure that your building receives a gentle flow of qi energy and that you are protected from 'poison arrows'. These are created when qi moves very fast along a straight roadway or when sharp angles from the roof lines or design elements of neighboring buildings hit your building. It is particularly inauspicious if these angles are directed towards your main entrance.

It is wise to check whether your main entrance is affected by poison arrows. Although there may be a number of entrances and exits in your building, qi only enters the building through the front entrance. It is also wise to check that the door of the main entrance is in proportion to the rest of the building; that is, neither too big nor too small for the qi to flow freely and gently. An entrance that is too large may mean loss of money, while a front door that is too small may constrict the flow of beneficial energy into the building, leaving the owner or tenants feeling impoverished.

Use the following checklist to identify potential problems from poison arrows aimed at your business. If you tick yes to any of the following questions, you

Checklist questions	Yes	No
Is your main entrance at the end of a straight street (at a T-intersection)?		
Is there a flagpole or a dead or misshapen tree directly opposite your main entrance?		
Is the angle of a triangular water feature directed towards the main entrance?		
Is there a pointed roof line directed at your main entrance?		

need to consider either moving your main entrance or blocking the path of the poison arrows with a softly curved sculpture, a water feature or some well-placed trees or shrubs. Revolving doors, an arch or a traffic roundabout can also help diffuse the flow of negative energy.

Traditionally, it was believed that living in an area where the streets all run parallel to each other in a grid formation caused bad feng shui, but now only busy thoroughfares are believed to be bad feng shui. Even the fast-flowing energy of these thoroughfares can be remedied to a certain extent by planting trees along the sides of the street.

Buildings in general have a predominantly yang energy. The bigger your workplace, the more important is it to balance the forcefulness of yang energy with softer yin energy. Yin energy is contained in the landscaping around the building. It is most auspicious to have a park near a large building, preferably with a fountain or other water feature in the middle.

CHINESE GOOD LUCK STREET NUMBERS

~

2 - EASY SUCCESS
5 - GOOD LUCK
6 - GOOD PROFITS
8 - GOOD BUSINESS
9 - HAPPY PROMOTION
10 - DESERVED CONFIDENCE

WORKPLACES TO AVOID

It is prudent to avoid working near areas or in buildings that have a poor balance of yin and yang energy. Buildings correspond with yang energy and landscaping corresponds with yin energy. Look at whether the building and the landscaping are in balance with each other. Also look at the design of the building – does it have sharp or precipitous design features, like a steep roof line or downward pointing arrows? Even if it doesn't, is it surrounded by such buildings? If so, you may find that the tenants or owners of the building are suffering from declines in profit, poor business and low morale.

When going for job interviews, take note of how you feel in the building (see also pages 70–71). If a building gives you a feeling of discomfort and oppression, you should consider carefully whether you really want to work there. If possible, ask to have a look at the offices or to be shown around generally. See the checklist on pages 44–45 to assess the flow of energy in this workplace. Similarly, if you are involved in locating your business, take how you feel about the place into consideration.

Workplaces such as schools, stock exchanges and buildings with a lot of machinery contain a lot of yang energy and can cause people working in the environment to feel constant, low-level anxiety unless there is a good counterbalance of yin energy, such as potted plants and the use of dark colors or dark woods for wall paneling or furniture. If you do work in such an environment, take care to spend weekends and holidays away in the country or on the water, to help revive your energy. There is an old feng shui saying that if you have bad luck, you should travel over water to wash it away.

EXPERT ADVICE

Try the following solutions:
• If you work near a railway, place a large earthenware pot outside your main entrance.
• If you work near an airport, incorporate a large external sculpture to hold down the energy or use big, heavy paperweights when you are working.

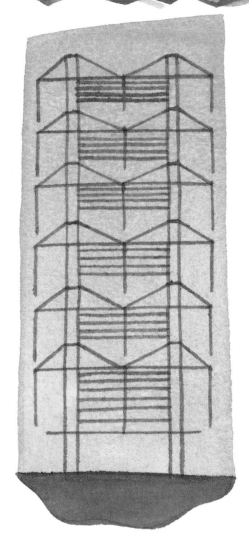

Places that are excessively yin in energy are frequently associated with death, grieving and other feelings of distress. It is best to avoid working near churches, graveyards and police stations. Working near sewerage installations and garbage dumps also encourages negative energy to enter your workplace.

EXPERT ADVICE

Try the following solutions:
• If you work near a police station, use peach colors with a little yellow in the decor of your business.
• If you work near sewerage outlets or garbage dumps, plant flowering trees and bright fragrant flowers near your main entrance.
• If you work near an undertaker, place a water feature outside your main entrance.

THE WORKPLACE INTERIOR

~

THE SHAPE OF YOUR BUILDING'S INTERIOR

Aim for balance, harmony and symmetry within your workplace or office. Rooms with a regular shape are particularly auspicious, according to feng shui beliefs. Also, when decorating, remember to have even numbers of decorative objects or pictures. Items in twos, fours or sixes are often arranged symmetrically and are considered much better than having an odd number of objects on your table or shelves.

If the building contains L-shaped rooms, take particular care with the prominent corner within the room and consider applying one of several cures to the corner or subdividing the room into two, as the prominent corner creates a poison arrow in a path diagonally across from the corner.

Place a leafy potted plant in the corner and one at the point where the diagonal hits the opposite wall. You may also wish to hang some chimes or a clear crystal in front of the corner. The danger of the corner can be further lessened by placing a mirror on the wall on either side of the corner. You should also make sure that the flow of qi is not stagnant in any alcoves. Stagnation can be avoided by placing a colorful lamp, perhaps a Tiffany-style, lead glass lamp, in the alcove.

Proportion is another important aspect to take into consideration. Make sure that the pieces of furniture you use in the offices or boardroom

EXPERT ADVICE

A well-known plumber was having difficulties with his business. Nothing seemed to work and he and his team experienced delays and client dissatisfaction. There were three dishwashers in complete disrepair standing near the entrance of his shop. Once he got rid of them, the plumber found that his business began to run smoothly again.

are in proportion with the space and ceiling height of the room. Overly large pieces of furniture, such as your desk, may introduce a more aggressive yang energy than the room can balance with yin space. You should also use furniture that echoes the shape of the room; for instance, two rectangular armchairs for a rectangular office rather than square, tub-shaped chairs.

Remember to avoid cluttering the space. Concentrate on keeping your storage area well organized, and if you do not have enough space for all your stock or files, consider having some of your storage off-site. You will enhance the flow of profit in your business if you observe this principle. If clutter continues to accumulate despite your best efforts, hang a clear quartz crystal over the jumble and allow its energies to help clear the space. If you get a lot of clutter through the mail, consider hanging out a 'No Junk Mail' sign near your postbox.

THE RECEPTION AREA:
THOSE IMPORTANT FIRST IMPRESSIONS

The reception area must be well positioned and decorated to enhance the full potential of your business, because it is the first area to receive the enhancing qi energy. It is important that the area is designed to encourage the flow of energy through to the rest of the building and that any potentially harmful poison arrows are blocked.

The person at the reception desk is essential to the organization. He or she has been employed to present a welcoming and efficient persona to clients and gives a very important first impression to people approaching the business. It is imperative that the receptionist is not sitting directly opposite the main entrance. This is because the qi rushes in through the main entrance and hits the reception desk, giving the receptionist a sense of unease and lack of focus, as well as a predisposition to headaches. This is intensified if a poison arrow is also pointing at the receptionist. Poison arrows are often caused by sharp design features of neighboring buildings that aim arrows towards the main entrance, by a straight road leading directly to the main entrance or by a tower or pole opposite it.

There are a number of ways of deflecting arrows outside the main entrance door (see pages 32–33), such as leaving a strong light on permanently at your main entrance. However, there are some solutions that can be implemented within the reception area, such as placing pieces of rounded furniture and plants in front of the receptionist or installing a statue or sculpture that features gentle curving lines. Rounded curves cause the energy to slow down, as it has to move around the object in its path.

You can deflect negative energy in a reception area by placing a mirror or a representation of the bagua mirror (see pages 26–27) above the main entrance. To allow the energy to move further into the building, the reception area

EXPERT ADVICE

Keep your indoor plants healthy. To increase wealth, place a coin in the soil of your potted plant. Popular indoor plants for prosperity include the 'money plant' (otherwise known as a dracaena), an evergreen which thrives well indoors.

It is imperative that the receptionist does not sit directly opposite the main entrance to an organization.

should have some curves that encourage the energy to flow around it and through to the work space behind.

Never allow your reception area to be a dark, overly yin room, as this can cause feelings of depression and unease. Place an even number of floor lamps that spread their light upward in the corners of the area and use potted plants with red, orange or yellow flowers. Choose lamps that are well rounded and even 'fat'. Avoid light fittings and lamps with sharp, angular design elements.

THE PLACEMENT OF AMENITIES

You should take account of where such amenities as the bathroom, kitchen and toilet are placed to prevent them from draining away profits. Work out where your wealth sector is both at work and at home, and see if a bathroom, kitchen or toilet is positioned in the area (see pages 22–27). If they are, you may find that money never stays long in the business.

Wealth is linked with yin energy and the element of water. It follows that all areas in your workplace that use water, such as sinks, baths and toilets, must be in good working order and not blocked. Also make sure that you keep all drains and plug holes covered.

It is also inauspicious if these amenities are close to or within view of the main entrance and elevators, and it is unwise to have these amenities positioned on the next floor directly above your main entrance. If your office faces a toilet door, request that a screen and some plants are placed between your door and the toilet.

If the bathroom and toilet are inauspiciously placed, make sure that the doors to both rooms are always kept closed and that a mirror is placed over or on the doors to negate the presence of the rooms symbolically. It is also extremely important to keep the toilet seat lid closed when not in use and have a mirror glued to the top of the lid. If you flush the toilet with the lid up, you might as well flush away your money.

Even if the toilet or bathroom is windowless, resist leaving the doors open. If you are worried about ventilation, see if you can have some ventilation or fans installed, and place red ribbons or wind chimes in the room to keep beneficial energy moving in these areas, which are usually small and cramped. If your bathroom is dark, bring in as much light and as many bright colors as possible to balance the yin darkness and function of the bathroom. You may consider a skylight, a bright border of tiles or new, warmly colored towels to balance the energy in the bathroom.

One of the most auspicious areas of a kitchen is the stove. Corporate kitchens often only contain a sink, a refrigerator and appliances for heating up food. If you do have a stove in the kitchen, it is important that it is kept as clean as possible and that it is in good working order, because the state of the stove, a fire element, corresponds to the generation of business. Do not extinguish this 'fire' by having a water element, such as a sink, right next to the stove. For the best luck in business and finance, it is best for the stove to face in a southeasterly direction.

EXPERT ADVICE

It is important to keep the toilet seat lid closed when not in use. Also, if you flush the toilet with the lid up, you might as well flush away your money.

COPING WITH OPEN-PLAN OFFICES

Open-plan or general offices are spaces where two or more people work in the same room. Semi-private offices divided by screens can also be considered open-plan. Particular attention must be paid to the placement of desks and chairs in these types of offices. Feng shui considerations for individual offices are discussed on pages 44–45.

It is important that the office space, whether in an individual or general office, is a regular shape with no protruding corners, as these create poison arrows that can hit other staff members. If a person is in the line of a poison arrow, their work will suffer, with symptoms ranging from a high absentee rate to an inability to meet deadlines or come up with new ideas (see pages 36–37 for ways to deflect poison arrows).

When considering seating, it is important that staff members are made to feel comfortable. The first step is to protect them from poison arrows and the second step is to make sure that staff members are **not** seated with their backs to a door or an opening in the cubicle.

Corridors between cubicles, offices and general office space conduct qi through the various spaces and openings. For qi to benefit a person, they must be seated so that they are facing the point at which the qi enters. If they sit with their backs to an opening, they will feel as if they are in danger and may consequently feel defensive and suffer from low morale. Positioning a desk against a wall is also inauspicious because there is very little space for the qi to flow in front of the person at the desk.

In a general office, desks should **not** be placed facing each other. This is a confrontational arrangement and leads to bickering and arguments. It is best to place desks in an octagonal

EXPERT ADVICE

If you are in an open-plan office, it is best if you sit in a position (preferably in the southeast) so that you do not see the backs of your colleagues. If you cannot change the position of your desk, consider making a symbolic fence around you by, for example, placing a plant or filing cabinet on the side of your desk and getting a chair with a high back (symbolic of supportive mountains at your back).

arrangement. If you use this formation, make sure that the desks all have rounded corners so that poison arrows are not created by sharp angles on the tabletop.

Be wary of having your desk positioned at the end of a long, straight corridor or near the bottom of a staircase. Hang up some wind chimes to slow down energy that rushes along a corridor or flight of stairs. Choose wind chimes that sound melodious, as they can attract prosperous energy into the building, whether they are made from metal or wood.

If you sit where your colleagues can see your back, consider getting a high-backed chair to symbolize a supportive mountain behind you.

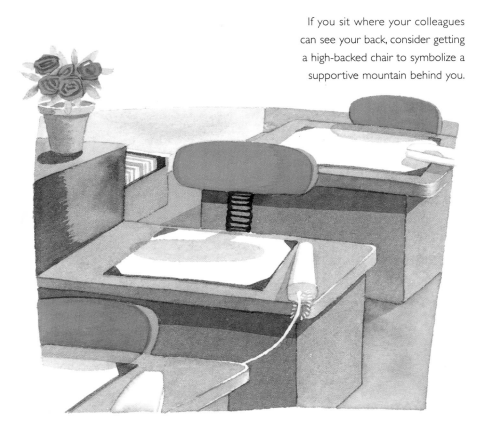

INDIVIDUAL OFFICE SPACE: EXECUTIVE SUCCESS

In an individual office (see pages 42–43), it is still important to position the desk correctly if you want to advance in your business and/or your job. Do not sit with your back to the door of your office. The optimum position for your desk is the corner diagonally opposite the door.

Check the proportions of your desk and make that your chair is comfortable and in proportion with the desk. In feng shui, there are auspicious and inauspicious measurements for important pieces of furniture, as well as for the windows and doors of your office. Check pages 52–53 for a table of auspicious measurements.

You may also like to align your desk with one of your lucky directions (see pages 62–65) or place it facing one of the following directions to encourage the following types of energy:

Direction	Energy
North	Motivated and successful
South	Relaxed and comfortable
East	Charismatic and authoritative
West	Inventive and efficient

Businesses thrive on communication. Make sure that the doors leading into the office are all in good working order. The doors are symbolic of strong communication of qi between managers and other members of staff. If the doors stick or are otherwise in disrepair, tension will mount within the department.

If your office is situated at the end of a long, straight corridor, consider placing a mirror or mirrored name plate on your door to deflect any poison arrows entering your office. If you have exposed beams protruding from the ceiling, make sure that your desk is not placed directly underneath them. Illnesses, ranging from mild headaches to serious diseases, can be caused by working under a beam. To defuse the strong destructive energy of the beam, tie two bamboo

flutes or wind chimes to the beam with red string. If possible, you may consider creating a false ceiling to hide the beams.

Decorate your office with bright yang colors, such as reds, oranges and yellows. Place plants in the corners of your office to prevent energy from stagnating in them. Consider placing a water feature between the door and the desk and hanging a picture of a mountain or a forest behind your head. The water feature symbolizes the free flow of money and business to your desk and the mountain symbolizes support for your business. You may like to put a picture of a beautiful river scene (not a waterfall) in front of you. Never hang a picture of a mountain in front of you, as this signifies obstacles and delays.

It is best to position your desk so your back is not to the door.

EXPERT ADVICE

If you travel a lot, hang a gray tassel in the northwest section of your home or workplace to ensure a safe journey, or carry a 2-inch Chinese coin with the inscription "Wish you safe wherever you go" with you. When staying at a hotel, hang a natural crystal in the window and lightly spray your own perfume or aftershave in the room to clear stagnant energies.

YOUR WORK BENCH, TABLE OR COUNTER

~

SIMPLE WAYS OF ENHANCING YOUR WORK PROSPECTS

If you work at a desk or other tabletop, apply some feng shui principles to your work table to improve your prospects. Choose the direction in which your work table faces according to the type of energy you want to attract (see pages 44–45), or make it face your lucky direction (see pages 62–65). Generally, it is favorable to sit facing the south or southeast direction to attract wealth and acknowledgment qi.

Try to make sure that you also sit facing the doorway or opening to your work space. However, you are often unable to move your office furniture to allow for feng shui. If this is the case and your back faces the entrance to your work space, you can cure this bad qi energy by placing a mirror on your tabletop so that the entrance is reflected in it.

Aspiration	Position on work table
Wealth	Top third, left-hand side
Acknowledgment	Top third, middle
Relationships	Top third, right-hand side
Health	Middle third, left-hand side
Creativity	Middle third, right-hand side
Knowledge (gaining a promotion)	Bottom third, left-hand side
Career	Bottom third, middle
Travel & mentors	Bottom third, right-hand side

There are some golden rules about work tables which you should observe:
• Keep your work table and space tidy for good flow of qi and for safety.
• Keep the drawers of your work table well organized.
• Use a work table that is auspicious in its measurements (see pages 52–53).

If you sit at a desk or use a countertop to make transactions with customers, you may enhance any of the eight aspirations (see pages 14–15) by mentally subdividing the tabletop into the following nine sections and placing good luck symbols in strategic places.

To encourage good fortune in these areas, place the following office equipment or good luck symbols in the appropriate area:

Office equipment	Good luck symbol
Cash register, calculator	Three coins tied together with red string
Certificates or diplomas of achievement, awards	Luo-pan compass (see pages 20–21)
Family or staff photo, telephone	African violets (Saintpaulia Confusa)
Lamp	Small piece of jade
Notebook	Small piece of opal
Reference books	The bagua with yin and yang symbol in the middle (see pages 26 -27)
Your work or computer	Black tassel
Telephone	Bagua with a convex mirror in the middle

THE IMPORTANCE OF KEEPING
YOUR WORK SPACE TIDY

Recognition, promotions and profit for yourself and the business can be encouraged by the state of your tabletop. Above all else, your desk must be absolutely clear of clutter. Remove all objects that are not in everyday use and keep your desk drawers tidy and functional.

Look at your work table and see whether there are any areas that are cluttered or corners that have been gathering dust. Keep your desk free of dust, as this symbolizes that you are keeping your work life free of stagnation.

Sometimes clutter arises because you do not have enough space. Consider extending your desk or workplace. However, be ruthless about what you actually need to keep – the more space you make, the more encouragement you give for beneficial qi to circulate through your work life. It is important not to push the clutter out of sight into cupboards or drawers, as this will just continue the stagnation of beneficial qi.

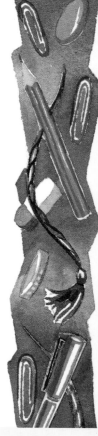

WORK BENCHES AND SAFETY

A work bench that has all the tools and hardware well organized will encourage beneficial qi into your work and will also help eliminate safety problems. Safety issues often arise because there is an improper flow of qi through crowded and inefficiently spaced benches and cluttered corridors.

Benches must be set at a height that is comfortable for you and the work that you do. The measurements of your work bench should also be auspicious (see pages 52–53).

If you are able to tap into the gentle flow of qi by organizing your work and work bench so that the energy flows to you at an easy, graceful pace, then you will find a corresponding benefit in your work life. You might begin to notice that any panic and last-minute deadlines disappear and work begins to flow at a steady and manageable rate, allowing you to do your best and gather recognition and other rewards.

EXPERT ADVICE

As workshops often have a lot of metal machinery or equipment with blades in them, make sure that you move any sharp edges of the machinery, saws or metal filing cabinets so that the sharp metal edges do not aim directly at your back. Also consider placing a water feature or picture of a placid river or calm sea between the wood and the metal elements in your workshop.

DESKS AND DRAWERS

Make sure that your desk or tabletop is in proportion to the room it is in and that it is not creating yang energy that is too strong. You may find that you suffer from headaches in the office if your desk is too big for your space or if the color of your desk is too strong; for example, black. Also avoid clear glass tabletops, as they signify lack of support.

It is preferable for your desk to be made of a hardwood timber, and the drawers should not stick. To create a sense of abundance, make sure that your drawers contain a generous amount of stationery and other equipment that you usually require for your work. This is not clutter if you use the supplies continually.

If you wish to attract wealth, clear any clutter and dust from the top left-hand side of your desk and consider placing one of these items on that part of the desk:

- A picture of brightly colored flowers or some brightly colored silk or wooden carved flowers
- The three-legged frog of fortune (siem choy)
- A small artificial jade tree
- A small, clear crystal ball

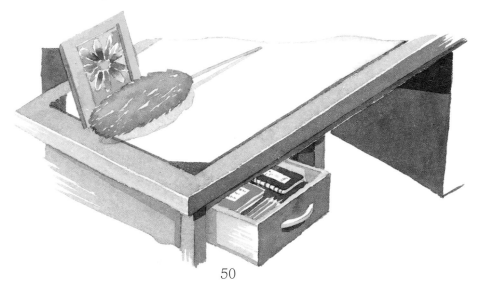

THE COUNTERTOP

As with desks, countertops must be a regular shape such as a rectangle, or a gently curved shape, and free from clutter. Measure the height, width and depth of the countertop and make sure that the edges of the countertop are not sharp and do not send poison arrows towards customers. If you run a retail clothing outlet, make sure that no poison arrows are shooting towards the changing room.

Countertops often display the cash register, and the cash register should be positioned in the wealth sector of your shop or at least on the top left-hand corner of the countertop.

It is unwise to place the cash register directly in line with the entrance of your shop. This can attract theft and burglary to the business. If you cannot move the cash register out of line with the entrance, place a potted plant with rounded leaves between the entrance and the cash register.

There are a number of symbols which invoke prosperity that you can place near your cash register to attract both new and continuing business. Place three coins tied with red thread or ribbon on your cash register, bank deposit book or telephone to attract deposits of unexpected abundance. Position a mirror behind or beside the cash register to double your earnings.

TABLE OF AUSPICIOUS AND INAUSPICIOUS MEASUREMENTS

In feng shui, all furniture and interior features, such as doors and windows, must be in correct proportion to the rest of the room. A feng shui ruler is used to measure these features. The ruler is subdivided into approximately 13mm or half-inch segments. The cycle repeats every 432mm or approximately 17 inches, and each segment corresponds to a particular meaning and is categorized as either auspicious or inauspicious.

The table opposite outlines auspicious and inauspicious segments of the feng shui ruler and the associated meanings of each segment. If your desk is an inauspicious height, consider replacing the legs to raise or lower the tabletop. If you have raised the height of your desk, you may find that you may be sitting a bit too low in your chair. Adjust your chair or get a slightly raised dais made which will bring your chair up to a height comfortable for you. Sitting on a dais also has the advantage of giving you a feeling of authority. If your window measurements are inauspicious, you can install curtains or blinds that are an auspicious size to mask your window.

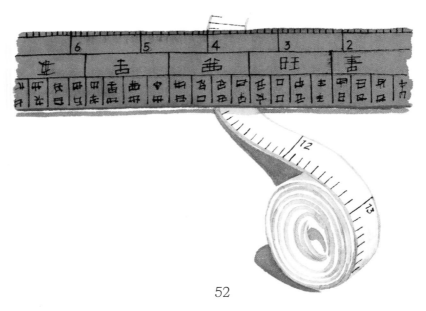

Measurement	Auspicious or inauspicious?	Meaning
0–2⅛ in 0–54mm	Auspicious	Money and abundance
2⅛–4 in 54–108mm	Inauspicious	Bad luck, legal difficulties & death in the family
4 in–6⅜in 108–162mm	Inauspicious	Bad luck, theft and loss of money
6⅜–8 in 162–215mm	Auspicious	Successful children and helpful people
8 –10⅝in 215–270mm	Auspicious	Honor and reward
10⅝–12 in 270–324mm	Inauspicious	Loss and disgrace
12–14⅞in 324–375mm	Inauspicious	Disease and scandal
14⅞–17in 375–432mm	Auspicious	Abundance

Expert Advice

One auspicious set of dimensions for a work desk or table is between 57 ³/₈–59 in (146.5–151cm) wide x 31 in–34 in (81–87cm) deep x 31 in–34 in (80–87cm) high.

WORK AND HOME

~

HOW THE DECORATION OF YOUR HOME
AFFECTS HOW YOU ARE SEEN AT WORK

In feng shui, not only do you have to know how to position and decorate your office or workplace for optimal success in your work life, but you must also pay attention to aligning your home with your work intentions.

The following principles, most of which you have already applied to your workplace, should also be applied to your home:

Principle	Reference to more information in this book
The house should be a regular shape.	See pages 28–29
The house should have mountains at the back of the building and a road or water feature at the front.	See pages 30–33
Qi or life energy should be allowed to flow around the exterior and interior of the house in gentle curves.	See pages 8–9; 38–39
There should be good balance between yin and yang energies.	See pages 10–11
There should be little or no clutter within the house.	See pages 18–19; 48
Your desk at home should be positioned so that your back is not facing the entrance to your bedroom and home study.	See pages 42–27
The measurements of main pieces of furniture and, particularly, the front door should be auspicious.	See pages 52–53
You should ensure that you suit your house and workplace.	See pages 62–65

The following pages describe how you can stimulate certain aspects of your work life at home. This is particularly useful if you have found that certain unlucky aspects of your workplace cannot be rectified; for example, if you cannot move your desk to avoid sitting with your back to the entrance of your work space. The following relevant aspirations can be stimulated in the appropriate areas of your home:

Relevant aspiration	Page number of this book	Compass direction
Stimulating your career	Page 56	North
Getting more money	Page 57	Southeast
Attracting attention	Page 58	South
Finding a mentor	Page 59	Northwest

See pages 22–27 on how to calculate which part of your home corresponds with each of the eight aspirations (see also pages 14–15). Tips for home offices can be found at pages 60–61.

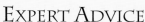

Expert Advice

If you want to enhance an aspiration in the relevant area in your home or workplace, a simple solution is to keep a light on in that area for at least two or three hours during the evening. As general principles:
- Keep light fittings in good order.
- Change lightbulbs when necessary.
- Keep lightbulbs covered with lamp shades or other suitable fittings.

HOW TO STIMULATE YOUR CAREER

The section of your house which corresponds to the career aspiration can be activated by feng shui remedies to boost your potential for career promotion, recognition and success. If you live in shared accommodation, find the area of your room that corresponds to your career (see pages 22–27)

The career area resonates with the element of water. If you feel overlooked or demoralized at work, place a small water feature inside your house or room, such as a bowl of water with brightly colored flowers floating on top. As the element of water is contained and given form by the element of metal, also place some decorative brass or silver-colored objects, such as metal picture frames, in this area, while avoiding any decorations that belong to the earth element, such as ceramic plates or pots.

Remember to clear any clutter from this area and, if you are going to an important meeting where you wish to make a good impression, place an object that represents your element (see pages 12–13) in this area. If your element is earth, you can still place an earth object in this part of your home because your personal element has a stronger energy than the general flow of elements and will attract success to you. Other objects that you can place in this area to stimulate success include the following:

• A picture of a coiled dragon; ensure that you do not place this before an entrance or doorway.

• A picture of an eagle, which should be placed before a window or door.

56

HOW TO DRAW IN MORE MONEY

There a great many symbols that you may place in the wealth area of your home to stimulate your fortunes and the success of your business. (To identify your wealth area, see pages 22–27.) Remember to clear clutter from the area to allow for an unimpeded flow of energy.

Many feng shui symbols of good luck are gold-colored. The coloring may be either artificial or natural. Gold-colored vegetables and fruit, such as pineapples and oranges, are examples of natural gold symbols. A tank of goldfish is also considered auspicious if placed in the wealth sector of your home (and business). No matter which symbol you choose to use, the object must always be placed in a elevated position. Never place these objects on the floor or at a low level, such as on a coffee table.

The wealth section corresponds with the element of wood, which means that this area may be stimulated with plants with rounded leaves and the use of light greens and tans in the decor. Although metal is generally harmful to wood, it is beneficial to place three coins wrapped in red paper under a potted plant in this area. Use wooden frames for your pictures in this area and also incorporate objects that correspond with the element of water, because this element nourishes the element of wood. However, if there are any sinks or toilets in this area, see pages 40–41. It is important to prevent opportunities for financial success from draining away.

Many feng shui symbols of good luck are gold-colored. Pineapples and oranges are examples of natural gold symbols.

57

HOW TO ATTRACT ATTENTION

The area of your home that corresponds to acknowledgment and fame can be stimulated by using objects corresponding to the element of fire. This would be an excellent area to place an even number of candles. However, it is best to avoid placing four of any object here or in any other area. In the Chinese language, the sound for 'four' is very similar to the word for 'death' and it is assiduously avoided in both street addresses and company logos.

The energy of the element of fire is enhanced by placing items in this area that are related to wood or plants. Choose wooden furniture with a reddish color, such as mahogany, for this area, as well as picture frames and lamp bases made of wood. Avoid water features in this area. If any of your amenities, such as the laundry or toilet, are in this area, hang or glue a mirror directly on the door on the side facing the corridor. The mirror creates an illusion that the rooms are not really there.

EXPERT ADVICE

Place the image of the 'Imperial Dragon' on the left-hand side of your desk to improve your position at work.

FINDING A MENTOR

If you feel surrounded by unscrupulous people at work or that you are staying in one place for too long, you may wish to stimulate the flow of energy in the mentor/travel area of your house or room.

To increase your opportunities to meet people who can help you in your business or to gain contracts that will involve more travel and further opportunities to meet helpful people, you need to enhance the elements of metal and earth. Place wind chimes in this section of your home or room. You may also include your stereo system somewhere in the room.

Also include objects that reflect the light in this area, such as clear rock crystals, glass ornaments or mirrors. Use a mirror in this area if it can be positioned to reflect a pleasant outlook, either internally or externally. Also include pictures of people enjoying themselves, and incorporate some yellow or gold in the color of the curtains or use these colors in some tassels which can be hung in this area, preferably from a window. Avoid objects that correspond to the element of fire, such as candles.

TIPS FOR THE HOME OFFICE

The home office is best located in your wealth, acknowledgment, career, mentor or knowledge areas. To work out where these aspirations fall within your home, see pages 22–27. Special decorations to stimulate your fortune, attract attention and helpful people are found on the following pages.

- To stimulate the wealth aspiration, see page 57.
- To stimulate the acknowledgment aspiration, see page 58.
- To stimulate the career aspiration, see page 56.
- To stimulate the mentor aspiration, see page 59.

The knowledge aspiration concerns not only obtaining knowledge (for passing examinations, for example); it also helps you to counter being overlooked at work due to under-qualification. This area corresponds to the element of water and is enhanced by metal. It is best kept free of objects and ornaments that correspond to the earth element.

However, although a piece of natural crystal may be thought of as an earth element, it is in fact a cure that can stimulate beneficial qi in any area of your home and office. You can stimulate your business acumen by placing a naturally pointed clear crystal or cluster of clear crystal in each corner of your home office.

Home offices for people who work predominantly for themselves must follow the same principles as offices in the workplace (see a summary of feng shui principles at pages 54–55), as must the positioning of the desk or work table (see pages 46–53).

In your home office, make sure that your furniture is in proportion to the office space, and do not have your work space in your bedroom where it may interfere with your sleep. Working at home has the disadvantage that it is often difficult to confine your job to normal working hours because of deadlines or expectations. Position your home office somewhere separate from your relaxation areas. If your office is not in a separate room, ensure that there is a clear division between your work and home space, using screens and potted plants.

Auspicious measurements for office furniture

Bookcases	108cm high, 89cm long and 38cm deep or 190cm high, 147cm long and 42cm deep
Office chair	seat should be 58cm high from the ground and the top of the chair back should be 81cm from the ground
Desk and work table	see pages 52–53

If you have open bookcases in your home office, consider placing glass or solid doors on them to shield you from the poison arrows created by the horizontal lines of the shelving. If you sit with your back to an open bookcase, you may feel that people are talking about you behind your back. To counter this, hang a six-coin charm from the back of your chair.

If you are a freelancer working from home, there are a number of useful things you can do to encourage work to flow to you. Hanging a faceted clear quartz crystal over the telephone or the fax machine will stimulate work-related calls. To stimulate new business, place a red tassel in the wealth corner of your home office.

EXPERT ADVICE

If you are constantly trying to meet deadlines, make sure that your clock is **not** facing the main entrance or front door. You do not want time to run out on you!

PERSONAL FENG SHUI

~

WHAT IS YOUR LUCKY DIRECTION?

Good fortune, an increased salary, job promotion and general happiness at work can be stimulated in your favor if you place your desk so that it faces a compass direction favorable to you. Each person has either an easterly or westerly orientation, and this gives them four compass directions which are personally favorable. Follow the directions below to find out your favorable direction. The following calculations will also help you work out your orientation or, if you want a shortcut, see pages 78–79 for the correspondence between your year of birth and your favourable orientation.

Step 1: Getting the remainder
Add together the digits of the year of your birth; for example, if it is 1963, you should add 1 + 9 + 6 + 3 to get a total of 19. Divide the total by 9, so in our example, this would be 19 divided by 9, giving you a resulting number of 2 and a remainder of 1.

Step 2: Getting your orientation number
• If you are **male**, *subtract* the remainder from 11; ie 11 - 1 = 10. If the resultant number is higher than 9, subtract 9 from the resultant number; ie 10 - 9 = 1.
•If you are **female**, *add* 4 to your remainder; ie 1 + 4 = 5.

If you get 5 as your orientation number and you are female, change your number to 8 and, if you are male, change your number to 2. This is because five (the number of the Chinese elements and the middle number of the magic square) is reserved for the number symbolizing earth.
If your calculation results in zero, choose 9 itself as your orientation number.

Step 3: What does your orientation number mean?

If you get 1, 3, 4 or 9, your orientation is east and the following directions are favorable:

- East
- Southeast
- South
- North

It follows from our example that a male person born in 1963 has an eastern orientation. He would experience a good flow of beneficial energy at work if his desk and the entrance to his workplace were facing east. However, a female person born in 1963 has a western orientation.

If you get 2, 6, 7 or 8, your orientation is west and the following directions are favorable:

- West
- Northwest
- Southwest
- Northeast

Be careful if your birthday falls at the beginning of the year, and check the Chinese calendar to see whether your year of birth is really the previous year by Chinese reckoning (see pages 78–79). For example, if you were born on 5 January 1965, your year of birth is 1964, because the Chinese year of 1964 ends on 1 February 1965.

DO YOU SUIT YOUR WORKPLACE?

There is a school of feng shui thought that also categorizes the orientation of buildings as either eastern or western. Once you know your personal orientation (see pages 62–63), you can work out whether you suit the orientation and corresponding energy of your workplace.

The concept is quite simple: eastern-oriented people are more comfortable and productive in eastern-oriented buildings, while western-oriented people are better suited to western-oriented buildings. If you spend a lot of time in a home or place of business that does not correspond with your orientation, you may experience demotion, unhappy work relationships or accidents.

To find out the orientation of your place of work, follow the exercise on pages 24–25. If you find using a compass difficult, check the position of your building with a map which shows compass directions.

Depending on how your building is sitting, you can determine whether the building is east- or west-oriented. If the back of your building is facing one of the following compass directions, it is an east-oriented building:

- North
- East
- Southeast
- South

4	9	2
3	5	7
8	1	6

If the building has an eastern orientation, the numbers 1, 3, 4 and 9 are favorable as they relate respectively to the compass directions of north, east, southeast and south.

This information also corresponds to your lucky areas in the workplace. If placed over a plan of your workplace, the grids on these pages will show you which areas in the building are lucky for you – those shaded purple are unlucky, while those shaded blue indicate your lucky areas.

If the back of your building is facing one of the following compass directions, it is a west-oriented building:

- Southwest
- Northwest
- West
- Northeast

4	9	2
3	5	7
8	1	6

If the building has a western orientation, the numbers 2, 6, 7 and 8 are favorable, as they relate respectively to the compass directions of southwest, northwest, west and northeast.

The corresponding lucky areas for people of western orientation are shaded blue while their unlucky areas are shaded purple.

If you are not compatible with your workplace, do not despair. This knowledge may help you understand why you may be having some trouble at, or dissatisfaction with, your work. To remedy such incompatibility, consider one of three options:

- Set up a home office.
- Make sure that your desk is facing one of your four favorable directions.
- Find an entrance to the building that is facing one of your four favorable directions and use this instead of the main entrance.

COMPATIBILITY WITH YOUR WORK COLLEAGUES

In feng shui, there are several ways of ascertaining whether you are compatible with a colleague or employer. A number of methods are based on a person's year of birth according to the Chinese calendar year (see pages 78–79) and whether they are male or female.

One of the simplest methods is to find out which of the five Chinese elements you and your work colleagues correspond to by following the table on page 13. The circle and five-pointed star formation of the elements on pages 12–13 give a guide to how the elements interact with each other. The table below lists which elements are compatible with each other.

Your element	Constructive elements (High compatibility rating)	Destructive elements (Low compatibility rating)
Earth	Earth, Fire, Metal	Wood, Water
Metal	Metal, Earth, Water	Wood, Fire
Water	Water, Metal, Wood	Fire, Earth
Wood	Wood, Water, Fire	Earth, Metal
Fire	Fire, Earth, Wood	Metal, Water

As there are five combinations of people that experience difficulties, try to off-set some of the negative effects of the combination by infusing your relationship with goodwill and by including a balancing element in the relationship area of your office or desk. For example, if you correspond to the wood element and the person you have difficulties with corresponds to the metal element, place a water element feature, such as a small bowl of water and very fresh flowers or a fish tank, in the relationship corner of your work space. The relationship corner is illustrated on the grid below:

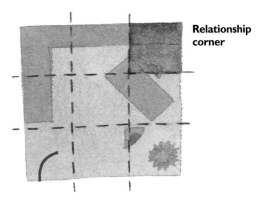

Relationship corner

Another simple method of checking your compatibility with others is to work out your work colleagues' orientations (see pages 62–63). Are they east or west? The most harmonious work relationships occur between people of the same orientation.

If you employ staff or are a manager of a group of staff members, it would be worthwhile to work out the elemental correspondences and east/west orientation of your work group. Make a note of who seems to get on with whom. You might be surprised by how feng shui calculations explain camaraderie between some staff members and animosity between others. For ways to improve poor working relationships, see pages 75–76.

PRACTICAL PROBLEM SOLVING

~

Apart from following the general feng shui principles outlined in this book (see pages 54–55 for a summary), there are a number of ways of helping your business cope with the usual daily struggles. It is important to remember that feng shui is not to be used in place of hard work and experience. However, feng shui principles and the techniques employed by feng shui practitioners tap into a wisdom that is based on ancient observations of nature. To take notice of this wisdom may help you align your business and lifestyle with the universal, natural energy that flows all around us.

MEETING A BUDGET

Feng shui methods of increasing wealth for your business and profits for you and your work colleagues often involve the use of coins and water. To meet your budget, consider one of the following strategies:

• Place a Chinese good luck coin in a red envelope and tape it to your cheque book or book of accounts.

• Place an eight-coin charm inside your book of accounts.

• Keep a piece of citrine in the wealth section of your work table.

• Place a pair of small figurines called 'lucky cats' by the cash register.

• Use a small figurine called Lin Hai who carries an oversized coin and a peach, symbolizing a long and fruitful business.

ATTRACTING CUSTOMERS

Two of the most effective ways of attracting customers to your business is through exterior signs and the placement of advertisements. Apart from applying the usual feng shui principles to your workplace (see pages 36–37), it is important that both signs and advertisements are auspicious in dimension (see pages 52–53).

Above all, your shop, as well as the signs and advertisements that you use, must be attractive to look at. Avoid decor and design that appear badly thought out. Hints of gold, expansive yang colors and a good lighting system should be used in both your business decor and any signs. In feng shui, neon signs are considered very auspicious because the light attracts beneficial qi.

There are numerous feng shui considerations for business signs. The sign should be well proportioned with a good balance of design elements (yang) and space (yin). It must be securely positioned and it should not cast a shadow on your main entrance or windows. It is auspicious to use either three or five colors in the sign, symbolizing growth and balance respectively. Never incorporate a prominent image of a four, as the word for four sounds like the word for death in Chinese, or a triangle, which is the symbol for fire and destruction.

If you are cementing the entrance to your premises, bury six coins leading up to your main entrance before the cement has been poured. If you have a mat outside your main entrance, place nine coins under it to attract customers to your door.

YOUR JOB INTERVIEW

Job interviews always seem one-sided, with the potential employer having the upper hand. However, by using the situation as an exercise in feng shui you will feel more empowered. Use your job interview as an opportunity to deduce a number of important facts about the business (see also pages 34–35) and this will help you work out whether you really want to work there.

If you are nervous about the job interview, carry a small brass goat or a small black tassel in your pocket with you into the interview. Take a black briefcase with metal clasps to which you could unobtrusively tie your black tassel. Black is symbolic of strength and perseverance.

If you can, evaluate the position of the building you are visiting and, if you have a good sense of direction and some time before the interview, roughly work out which compass direction the windows of the room face. When in the interview room, try to sit facing one of your lucky directions (see pages 62–63). If you are unable to work this out, simply make sure that you do not have your back to the entrance to the room.

EXPERT ADVICE

On the morning of the interview, take some time to clear out your briefcase, wallet or handbag completely, symbolizing the clearing out of old energies to make way for the new. If you are driving to the interview, also clear your car of clutter.

CONDUCTING AN EFFECTIVE BOARDROOM MEETING

When making preparations for an important boardroom meeting, take some time to work out the seating arrangements. The person who is conducting the meeting or who is your key negotiator should be seated in what is called 'the honored guest position', which is the chair most visible from the doorway. That person should also be facing one of their lucky directions (see pages 62–63).

Make sure that the view from the chair is pleasant and does not include doorways to the bathroom/toilet. For a very important meeting, place a screen and some potted plants in the room in front of the entrance to the boardroom to shield the person who must sit with their back to the door.

The boardroom table should be in proportion with the boardroom and should be made of hardwood timber. To generate friendly relations, the table top must be circular, oval or octagonal. In feng shui, square tables are not auspicious, as the poison arrows created by the sharp points of the corners can create arguments and may leave negotiations unresolved. If you have a square table, place a circular or octagonal centerpiece in the middle of the table to divert some of the poison arrows. Place a large round decorative object, such as a large crystal bowl, on the table to generate harmony and good communication. Also, always invite an even number of attendees to the meeting. The boardroom table should be in proportion with the boardroom; one auspicious height for such a table is 80cm. It must accommodate an even number of people, and it is advisable to invite an even number of attendees to the meeting.

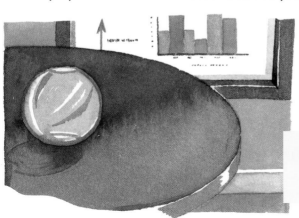

EXPERT ADVICE

A good position for the boardroom is in the knowledge part of the building.

SETTING UP OR RELOCATING YOUR BUSINESS

When setting up or relocating your business, take the feng shui principles discussed at pages 28–35 into consideration. If you are relocating because you are expanding your business, consider some important points raised on page 77.

No matter what, be sure to find out what happened to the previous owners of the premises. If they relocated because they were expanding or the owners retired after a long and successful work life, the premises are more than likely to be auspicious. If the previous owners or tenants went bankrupt, suffered from embezzlement, low morale or high turnover of staff, or failed to pay their rent or mortgage on time, it is best to avoid these premises.

It is considered most auspicious to open your business after the new moon. In the Chinese calendar, each day is categorized as lucky or unlucky. To find out whether the day your business started was lucky or to schedule a date for the start of your business, an English version of an important Chinese almanac, the Tong Shu, is available every year. This almanac also lists lucky and unlucky times of the day.

President or founder of the business	wealth sector
Reception	relationship sector
Staff room	creativity sector
Boardroom	knowledge sector
Accounting department	career or knowledge sector
Sales department	career or relationship sector
Marketing	acknowledgment/fame sector
Amenities	health/family sector

CHANGING YOUR BUSINESS NAME OR LOGO

In the Chinese business world, the auspiciousness of a company's name is determined by the number of strokes taken to write it in Chinese characters. This is not really applicable in the West; however, there are still some important feng shui principles which should be observed for Western business names. Names chosen for a business should be appropriate and should include words with positive connotations or that are uplifting or inspiring. In China, many business names include words such as 'happy' or 'lucky'. Be careful also with words that sound similar to negative words, such as 'death', 'hate' or 'forgotten'.

Logos are an integral part of your business and great consideration must be given to having a well-balanced and appropriate design. Designs that are considered auspicious are those that incorporate fluid, gently curving lines, which symbolizes the beneficial flow of qi and is reminiscent of the sinuous lines of the dragon. The incorporation of a fat and happy dragon in a logo is especially fortunate.

Some lucky images include upright arrows. Arrows that point downwards are inauspicious and should be avoided, as should crosses, as they symbolize problems and strife. If you have designed a vibrant symbol, it is inauspicious to enclose it with a circular border, as this symbolizes the constriction of energy. Otherwise, the circle is an auspicious sign, as it symbolizes heaven, and so is the square, as it symbolizes earth.

First and foremost, if your company is undergoing retrenchment and reshuffles, make absolutely sure that you place your desk facing your lucky direction (see pages 62–63) and that your back is **not** facing the entrance to your work space. Also check that there are no poison arrows directed at you by the sharp corners of desks, bookshelves, partitions or walls.

If there are sharp arrows pointed at you or if your back is to the entrance, place a small mirror on your desk and position it so that you are deflecting the poison arrows or are able to see the entrance of your work space without turning around.

There are a number of useful objects, such as a figurine or picture of a bear, that symbolize protection in feng shui. You can place these objects in the career area of your workplace or hang the picture at the back of your work chair (particularly if your back is to the entrance of your work space).

A useful object to place on your desk is the figure of the Monkey God. If you cannot get this object, see if you can find a drawing or picture of one which can be photocopied and placed on your desk near where you usually sit or near your telephone, computer monitor or equipment that you use frequently during your work hours.

EXPERT ADVICE

Place a paperweight over your papers or files, symbolizing that you and your work are firmly entrenched and will not be moved.

COPING WITH A DIFFICULT BOSS OR WORK COLLEAGUE

Some of your difficulties with a supervisor, manager or work colleague may be understood by working out the elements and orientations you and your co-worker resonate with (see pages 62–63; 66–67), using feng shui calculations. As you can see from page 13, each type of person works in different ways and has different parameters, some of which may seem oppressive to you.

The most difficult of bosses or work colleagues tend to be those who resonate with an element that is oppressive or destructive to your own. One way of countering personality differences and clashes is by placing an image of an element that acts as a shield against the hostility that is sometimes inadvertently aimed at you by your co-worker.

The following table lists your element, the corresponding destructive element and the balancing element; that is, the element that will shield you from the destructive one. Place an object that resonates with the balancing element in the relationship area of your work space or work table.

Your element	Destructive element	Balancing element
Wood	Metal	Water (glass of water that you drink)
Fire	Water	Wood (wooden frame with a photo of two people getting along happily)
Earth	Wood	Fire (red candle)
Metal	Fire	Earth (ceramic pot)
Water	Earth	Metal (brass figurine of an elephant, symbolic of peace and harmony)

WHAT TO DO ABOUT LOW PRODUCTIVITY

Low productivity and low morale seem to go hand in hand. It might be wise to work out the lucky orientation of each member of your staff (see pages 62–63). Working in a building that resonates for only some staff members can cause enormous difficulties and clashes. Also, check the elemental orientation between staff members, supervisors and managers. Solutions for people who are not naturally compatible can be found at page 75.

If a member of your workforce is feeling particularly hostile, there are two important things that you need to check to help make that person feel more comfortable. First, determine whether their entrance into the building should be changed. Ideally, the owner of the business and staff members should enter the building through the main entrance to encourage beneficial energy to circulate through the building. However, if the orientation of the entrance is not aligned with that of an individual, then alternative entrances should be investigated, such as entering through the car park. Second, make sure that the affected person's work table is facing one of their lucky directions.

EXPERT ADVICE

It is important that low morale is countered by the incorporation of yang features in your building's interior. This will increase feelings of expansiveness among the staff. Incorporate upward-facing lamps, large paintings, posters, and generously proportioned furniture in the workplace, and remove any broken furniture and out-of-date machinery.

PLANNING FOR THE FUTURE

When planning to expand in the future, be careful to take some of the feng shui principles in this book into account. Often, successful businesses that have thrived in one residence have suffered due to an over-extension of the business. For example, by placing an extension to a certain part of your building, you may be creating poison arrows that are directed straight to your sales team manager, in which case you may soon experience low morale issues from your sales force. Either move the sales team or consult a feng shui practitioner to make sure that you do not damage the energy flow of your business.

Extensions that are under a third of the length of the building are usually beneficial to the aspiration to which that area of the building corresponds. For example, if you build an extension on to your wealth area that is under a third of the length of the existing building, you will probably find that your business will go from strength to strength.

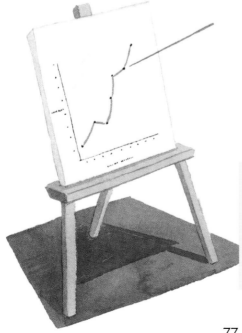

EXPERT ADVICE

If a business is expanding, it is wise not to let go of the premises that brought it luck. It is thought to be most auspicious if the lucky premises are kept and extra premises are taken nearby.

CHINESE CALENDAR

~

New year date	Element	Yin/Yang	Female (E/W)	Male (E/W)	New year date	Element	Yin/Yang	Female (E/W)	Male (E/W)
1919 Feb 1	Earth	Yin	West	East	1942 Feb 18	Water	Yang	West	East
1920 Feb 20	Metal	Yang	West	West	1943 Feb 5	Water	Yin	East	East
1921 Feb 8	Metal	Yin	West	West	1944 Jan 25	Wood	Yang	East	West
1922 Jan 28	Water	Yang	East	West	1945 Feb 13	Wood	Yin	West	East
1923 Feb 16	Water	Yin	East	West	1946 Feb 2	Fire	Yang	West	East
1924 Feb 5	Wood	Yang	West	East	1947 Jan 22	Fire	Yin	West	West
1925 Jan 24	Wood	Yin	East	East	1948 Feb 10	Earth	Yang	West	West
1926 Feb 13	Fire	Yang	East	West	1949 Jan 29	Earth	Yin	East	West
1927 Feb 2	Fire	Yin	West	East	1950 Feb 17	Metal	Yang	East	West
1928 Jan 23	Earth	Yang	West	East	1951 Feb 6	Metal	Yin	West	East
1929 Feb 10	Earth	Yin	West	West	1952 Jan 27	Water	Yang	East	East
1930 Jan 30	Metal	Yang	West	West	1953 Feb 14	Water	Yin	East	West
1931 Feb 17	Metal	Yin	East	West	1954 Feb 3	Wood	Yang	West	East
1932 Feb 6	Water	Yang	East	West	1955 Jan 24	Wood	Yin	West	East
1933 Jan 26	Water	Yin	West	East	1956 Feb 12	Fire	Yang	West	West
1934 Feb 14	Wood	Yang	East	East	1957 Jan 31	Fire	Yin	West	West
1935 Feb 4	Wood	Yin	East	West	1958 Feb 18	Earth	Yang	East	West
1936 Jan 31	Fire	Yang	West	East	1959 Feb 8	Earth	Yin	East	West
1937 Feb 11	Fire	Yin	West	East	1960 Jan 28	Metal	Yang	West	East
1938 Jan 31	Earth	Yang	West	West	1961 Feb 15	Metal	Yin	East	East
1939 Feb 19	Earth	Yin	West	West	1962 Feb 5	Water	Yang	East	West
1940 Feb 8	Metal	Yang	East	West	1963 Jan 25	Water	Yin	West	East
1941 Jan 27	Metal	Yin	East	West	1964 Feb 13	Wood	Yang	West	East

New year date	Element	Yin/Yang	Female (E/W)	Male (E/W)	New year date	Element	Yin/Yang	Female (E/W)	Male (E/W)
1965 Feb 2	Wood	Yin	West	West	1988 Feb 17	Earth	Yang	East	East
1966 Jan 21	Fire	Yang	West	West	1989 Feb 6	Earth	Yin	East	West
1967 Feb 9	Fire	Yin	East	West	1990 Jan 27	Metal	Yang	West	East
1968 Jan 30	Earth	Yang	East	West	1991 Feb 15	Metal	Yin	West	East
1969 Feb 17	Earth	Yin	West	East	1992 Feb 4	Water	Yang	West	West
1970 Feb 6	Metal	Yang	East	East	1993 Jan 23	Water	Yin	West	West
1971 Jan 27	Metal	Yin	East	West	1994 Feb 10	Wood	Yang	East	West
1972 Feb 15	Water	Yang	West	East	1995 Jan 31	Wood	Yin	East	West
1973 Feb 3	Water	Yin	West	East	1996 Feb 19	Fire	Yang	West	East
1974 Jan 23	Wood	Yang	West	West	1997 Feb 7	Fire	Yin	East	East
1975 Feb 11	Wood	Yin	West	West	1998 Jan 28	Earth	Yang	East	West
1976 Jan 31	Fire	Yang	East	West	1999 Feb 16	Earth	Yin	West	East
1977 Feb 18	Fire	Yin	East	West	2000 Feb 5	Metal	Yang	West	East
1978 Feb 7	Earth	Yang	West	East	2001 Jan 24	Metal	Yin	West	West
1979 Jan 28	Earth	Yin	East	East	2002 Feb 12	Water	Yang	West	West
1980 Feb 16	Metal	Yang	East	West	2003 Feb 1	Water	Yin	East	West
1981 Feb 5	Metal	Yin	West	East	2004 Jan 22	Wood	Yang	East	West
1982 Jan 25	Water	Yang	West	East	2005 Feb 9	Wood	Yin	West	East
1983 Feb 13	Water	Yin	West	West	2006 Jan 29	Fire	Yang	East	East
1984 Feb 2	Wood	Yang	West	West	2007 Feb 18	Fire	Yin	East	West
1985 Feb 20	Wood	Yin	East	West	2008 Feb 7	Earth	Yang	West	East
1986 Feb 9	Fire	Yang	East	West	2009 Jan 26	Earth	Yin	West	West
1987 Jan 29	Fire	Yin	West	East	2010 Feb 14	Metal	Yang	East	West

Published by Lansdowne Publishing Pty Ltd
Sydney NSW 2000, Australia

Publisher: Deborah Nixon
Production Manager: Sally Stokes
Text: Antonia Beattie and Rosemary Stevens
Illustrator: Sue Ninham
Designer: Sue Rawkins
Editor: Jocelyn Hungerford
Project Co-ordinator: Kate Merrifield

National Library of Australia Cataloguing-in-Publication-Data
    Beattie, Antonia.
    Feng Shui at work.
    ISBN 1 86302 718 1
    1. Feng-shui. 2. Quality of work life. I. Stevens, Rosemary, 1952-. II. Title.
    133.3337

Set in Stempel Schneidler on QuarkXPress
Printed in Singapore by Tien Wah Press (Pte) Ltd